Basic Interviewing Skills and Techniques:

A Workbook for Application

Victoria Venable
Salisbury University

Becky Anthony
Salisbury University

Basic Interviewing Skills and Techniques

ISBN:1533323070
ISBN-13: 978-1533323071

DEDICATION

To all the social work educators who are dedicated to making a difference by teaching others about the science of helping.

CONTENTS

ACKNOWLEDGMENTS

We would like to thank the students and faculty in the Department of Social Work at Salisbury University.

Lesson One

Social Work Ethics

Discussion 1.1 Ethics in General

Here is a brief breakdown of the National Association of Social Workers (NASW) Code of Ethics. For more detailed information go to the NASW website: www.socialworkers.org (NASW, 1999).

The Core Values and Principles from the NASW Code of Ethics

Service: Social workers are to help others and address social problems

Social Justice: Social workers are committed to advocating for change to assist the vulnerable and oppressed

Dignity and Worth of the Person: Social workers seek to empower and are respectful of all types of diversity

Importance of Human Relationships: Social workers collaborate and interact with others to facilitate change

Integrity: Social workers are honest and ethical in their practice

Competence: Social workers are lifelong learners in order to ensure that they provide well-informed services

Questions to Consider:

- What are ethics?

- How do our values influence our personal ethics?

- Why is an ethical code so important to a social work professional?

- What is an ethical dilemma?

- How can I identify the best course of action when faced with an ethical dilemma?

- In what situations could society's well-being or legal obligations override your commitment to a client?

- What are the LIMITS to confidentiality?

- How might advocating for a client put you in conflict with your agencies' polices or practices?

- What are some different ways you could evaluate your work?

- What is a population you are interested in working with? How could you advocate for change at each level?

Table 1.1*

Ethical Standards	What Does This Mean for You as a Social Work Student?
One: Social Workers' Responsibility to Clients	• Your priority in practice is the well-being of your client • Clients have the ability to make their own decisions unless they are at serious risk for harm • Clients need to fully understand what they are agreeing to do with a social worker • You must avoid having dual relationships with clients • You should always maintain a client's privacy and ensure that clients understand what confidentiality is • Engaging in a sexual relationship or in sexual activities with clients is never appropriate • You should work to prepare your clients to transition to a new worker before leaving your field placement
Two: Social Workers' Ethical Responsibility to Colleagues	• You should treat your coworkers with respect • It is always a good idea to seek advice and counsel from your coworkers on cases where they have relevant knowledge • Engaging in a sexual relationship or in sexual activities with coworkers is never appropriate. • When you believe that a coworker is impaired or behaving unethically, talk to them and/or a supervisor
Three: Social Workers' Ethical Responsibilities In Practice Settings	• You should always document your time in an accurate and timely manner • It is important to be sure that you uphold all commitments made to your employer/field placement • Advocate within the agency to improve policies or practices is important

Table 1.1 Continued

Ethical Standards	What Does This Mean for You as a Social Work Student?
Four: Social Workers' Ethical Responsibilities As Professionals	• It is important to practice within your area of developing knowledge and with appropriate supervision • Your practice cannot oppress or marginalize others • How you conduct your personal life should not keep you from meeting your professional obligations • You should never participate in fraud or deception
Five: Social Workers' Ethical Responsibilities To The Social Work Profession	• You should take the necessary steps to evaluate your work with clients
Six: Social Workers' Ethical Responsibilities To The Broader Society	• It is important to be knowledgeable about all systems that impact your clients (e.g. micro, mezzo, and macro) • You should be actively involved in change and advocacy in some form at all levels of practice

*Table adapted from National Association of Social Workers (1999). NASW Code of Ethics. Washington, DC: National Association of Social Workers.

Consider This! Read the scenario and consider the following questions:

Tara is a master's level social worker in a community mental health center in a small town in rural West Virginia. A man comes in with his son, who is depressed and said by the father to have been diagnosed with Tourette's Disorder. Tara knows a little about Tourette's and the complications its neurological tics can cause for the person, but she has never worked with anyone diagnosed with it. The nearest large hospital and counseling center is over 200 miles away, and the father says that, because of his work schedule, he cannot take his son there for help. He asks Tara to help him. What should she do?

1. Which standards, values, and principles from the Code of Ethics are related to this situation? (Cite specifically from the Code of Ethics)

2. What are the different choices that the social worker could make in this dilemma?

3. Who stands to gain and who (if anyone) stands to lose from each possible choice?

4. What would you do in this situation?

Application

EXERCISE 1.1: View the "An Ethical Dilemma: What Would you Do?" video in MyClasses Canvas and answer the following questions:

Option #1:

1. Based upon what you saw in the video as Option #1, do you think Camille reacted appropriately to her co-worker's issues? Why?

2. Based upon what you saw in the video as Option #1, is what Camille did supported by the NASW Code of Ethics? Why or why not?

Option #2:

1. Based upon what you saw in the video as Option #2, do you think Camille reacted appropriately to her co-worker's issues? Why?

2. Based upon what you saw in the video as Option #2, is what Camille did supported by the NASW Code of Ethics? Why or why not?

Option #3:

1. Based upon what you saw in the video as Option #3, is what Camille did supported by the NASW Code of Ethics? Why or why not?

Overall

If you were in Camille's situation, how would you have handled this ethical issue with your co-worker? Which option would you choose and why?

Many social work students utilize digital and social media technologies personally, and some will be asked to utilize them professionally. For professional social workers who utilize digital technologies, we need to be aware of the NASW Code of Ethics and professional standards around use of technologies. The following section provides suggestions for social work students who choose to utilize digital and social media.

Digital and Social Media Suggestions for Social Work Students

Digital devices are laptops, tablets, smart phones and any form of wearable technology. Social media are websites and applications that allow people to create and share content and/or participate in social networking.

Students in Social Work programs are expected to ethically use digital and social media. These suggestions are provided for students to help them better understand, if they choose to use new technologies, how best to utilize digital and social media in courses and in social work practice. Students are not required to have social media accounts and these suggestions are only applicable in cases where a student makes the decision to create a social media presence.

As social workers and educators we utilize ethical guidelines from the University (e.g. Salisbury University School of Social Work's Social Media & Digital Technology Policy), the National Association of Social Workers (NASW) Code of Ethics, the Family Education Rights and Privacy Act (FERPA), and the NASW & the Association of Social Work Boards (ASWB) Standards for Technology and

Social Work Practice. These ethical digital and social media suggestions are based around the social work concepts of maintaining boundaries, confidentiality, and integrity.

Social Work students will:

- Receive permission to friend or follow another student and/or professor

- Obtain permission from others who may be involved in or potentially impacted by videos, pictures, etc. before posting them on social media accounts

- Consider using and maintaining privacy settings on personal social media accounts

- Abide by copyright laws, Creative Commons Licensing and other ethical guidelines when citing the work of others

- Refrain from posting negative comments about matters related to the educational program (e.g. field placements, class work, etc.), students, or faculty on social media

- Respond to email messages in a timely, respectful, and efficient manner

In the classroom, students will:

- Bring and use digital devices for the sole purpose of taking notes and searching for course related content, if approved by the course instructor

- Keep all mobile phones, tablets, and other wearable devices on silent

- Alert the instructor prior to the start of class that there may be a situation where a phone call will need to be taken and ask for permission to leave class in order to answer the call

In the classroom, students will not:

- Use digital devices to do anything other than class related activities

- Answer phones, emails, or text messages during class sessions without advanced permission from the instructor

- Take or share photos without the permission of the instructor and/or the other students

- Record (audio or video) or share the recording of any activity in the class without the permission of the instructor and/or the other students

The best way to use email within courses and the social work department is to:

- Always use your university email address

- Be professional

- Include a greeting (if you do not know your professor's title (Dr., Mrs., etc.) please address them as professor), a brief discussion that includes why and what you are emailing about, and a sign-off with a signature line

- Use complete sentences and proper punctuation

- Do not use jargon, emoticons, or emojis

- Respond to emails from your instructor, advisor, and/or the department in a timely manner

Students need to realize that:

- Location-based services on social media and other sites may inadvertently divulge their whereabouts such as the location of the classroom on campus

- Posts and comments about classmates and professors on social media may not remain private and confidential

- Sites that allow users to rate their professors and/or University can also compromise a student's confidentiality

These guidelines were adapted from:

Hitchcock, L. (2016, February 12). My guidelines for using digital and social tech in the classroom and beyond. *Teaching and learning in social work [Blog]*. Retrieved from http://www.laureliversonhitchcock.org/2016/02/12/my-guidelines-for-using-digital-social-tech-in-the-classroom-and-beyond/

Application

EXERCISE 1.2: Read the scenario and answer the following questions:

Rashad is a BASW student who is interning at a local homeless shelter called *Open Arms*. One day at his internship he had a powerful conversation with one of the residents who is a Vietnam veteran. The man indicates that he has suffered with PTSD for many years and has abused drugs and alcohol to cope with his symptoms. The man also states that has no family and is often treated poorly by people on the street because of his appearance. Rashad is so moved by the conversation that he wants to capture the moment. He takes out his phone and snaps a pic of the man and his belongings but makes sure he doesn't get the man's face in the picture. At the end of the day, Rashad is talking to some of his friends about the problems with how veterans are treated in this country and decides to post his views on social media. Rashad's first post reads:

> *"Talked to a real hero at work today. Homeless yet he sacrificed everything for this country. America, our priorities are !*%@* up. #VETSlivesmatter #toughdayatwork"*

He then went to his other social media account and posted the pic of the man from his internship with the caption:

> *"This is what a real MAN, a real HERO looks like. All you other whiners and complainers trying to avoid your responsibilities need to wake the %$*^ up! Mental health is real and we need to make sure that programs like the OPEN ARMS agency keep their funding so that men like this don't get left on the streets. #VETSlivesmatter #socialworkadvocacy #socialworkersmustspeaktruth"*

Questions to Answer

1. What about Rashad's posts and actions were ethical or unethical? Professional or unprofessional?

2. What does the Code of Ethics say about actions like Rashad's? (Cite specific standards, values, and principles from the Code of Ethics)

3. What could be some of the unintended consequences that come from Rashad's posts?

4. In what ways can social workers utilize social media as professionals? How is the usage of social media as a professional different than how it is utilized in a social worker's personal life?

Lesson Two

Body Language and Non-Verbal Communication

Discussion

When working with clients it is important that we are aware of the different ways we send information to clients. It is also important to recognize what types of messages our clients are sending back to us during interactions. As a social worker we must be sure to speak slowly and clearly to our clients. In addition, we must avoid jargon, slang, using abbreviations or idioms (e.g. "This costs an arm and a leg!")

There are two major components that work together when we are communicating with clients. **Attending** and **Listening.** Attending involves paying attention and focusing your thoughts and attention (*psychological attending*) on the client and what they are saying. In addition to being focused, attending also involves presenting ourselves as though we are paying attention (*physical attending*). This means using the SOLER skills (Egan, 2014).

Listening is far more involved than simply hearing what the client is saying. Yes, we need to pay attention to what the client actually says (*verbal communication*) but a skilled social worker also makes note of the *non-verbal information* provided by the client.

Egan, Gerard. (2014). *The skilled helper: A problem management and opportunity development approach to ehling* (10th ed). Belmont, CA: Brooks/Cole.

Consider This! Can you tell what emotion each face is conveying?

Table. 2.1

CAN YOU NAME THE EMOTION?	
1._____ What information in the picture helped you make your decision?	
2._____ What information in the picture helped you make your decision?	
3._____ What information in the picture helped you make your decision?	
4._____ What information in the picture helped you make your decision?	

Application

EXERCISE 2: Review the *Intake Video* in MyClasses Canvas and identify the various SOLER skills and psychological attending. Next, complete the following questions related to the video:

1. What were the specific SOLER skills executed correctly by the social worker in the video?

2. How would you have executed any of the SOLER skills differently?

3. How well did the social worker demonstrate psychological attending in the video?

4. What were some types of nonverbal communication (e.g. metacommunication) that the client displayed during the interview?

5. What were some types of paralinguistic cues that the client displayed during the interview?

Lesson Three

Reflecting and Summarizing

Discussion

One of the most difficult tasks for beginning social workers is learning how to talk with a client and skillfully utilize questions. It is very tempting to engage a client by fact-finding and interrogating instead of simply exploring the client's feelings and the underlying content of what they are saying. This is why we will focus on the important skills of Reflecting and Summarizing before moving on to asking questions.

Reflecting and summarizing are all important aspects of listening that can help when effectively communicating with your clients. The following table gives you a brief breakdown on each of these skills.

Table 3.1

Skill	What is it?	Examples
Reflection of Feeling	Restating and exploring the client's feelings that are expressed verbally and nonverbally	• It sounds like you are feeling overwhelmed by.... • If I am hearing you correctly, you felt terrified when that car.... • It appears as though you are really excited about.....
Reflection of Content	A way to let the client know you are listening by repeating (briefly) back specific information or facts. It also can work as a means of fact checking with the client	• I hear you saying that you had a rough day yesterday after you lost your wallet. • I sense that you and your sister are in a better place today. • Correct me if I'm wrong, but you told your boyfriend to get lost after he came home late last night.

Table 3.1 Continued

Skill	*What is it?*	*Examples*
Summarizing	Pulling together major points and relevant pieces of information from the client's discussion and creating a consolidated response. This can incorporate both reflections of feeling and content. It can also be used intermittently during the client interview and is a good way to begin and end a session	Just as a recap, last week you talked about how happy you feel about reconnecting with your biological father. We discussed that you also felt some anger and resentment but largely you were excited to meet him again. You also talked about how important it is to you that he follow through with his promises about coming to your graduation.

Application

EXERCISE 3: You will need to review the *Intake Video* in MyClasses Canvas. Next, complete the process recording chart for the video and breakdown the usage of reflections and summarizing in the session. In your process recording you will need to identify the following skills and information:

- Reflection of content and feelings

- Summary

- Quality of the skill demonstrated (e.g., good, bad). Include what is was about the skill that made it good or bad.

- How was the skill useful in helping the worker engage or talk with the client?

- How would you have used the skill differently if you were conducting the session?

Lesson Four

Use of Questions

Discussion

Asking questions is very important and can feel like one of the easiest skills to master. Skillfully asking questions is actually a skill that has to be diligently worked on if a social worker wants to come across as caring and thoughtful. Many factors influence how a social worker uses questions and elaborations in conversations with clients. Some of those factors include the client's cultural identify, the client's thoughts and feelings, and the relationship between the social worker and the client.

Questions can be used during all stages of the working relationship but are heavily relied upon during engagement and assessment.

Table 4.1

Type of Question	What is it?	Example
Open	Allows for flexible responding and gives the client more control over the discussions	How did you feel about that? Where would you like to begin?
Closed	Provides more focus but does not give the client the opportunity to elaborate. Can usually be answered with one word or simple responses	Do you live alone? Did that make you sad?
Pseudo-question	These can often be a direction or suggestion disguised as a question	Don't you want to start on your homework? Aren't you too old to cry about that?

Table 4.1 continued

Type of Question	What is it?	Example
Tangential	These occur when the social worker is attempting to investigate or inquire about unrelated topics	**Client**: I was just at the mall and I was so freaked out by all of the people there. I don't think I'll go back any time soon! **Worker:** Oh wow! Did you get a chance to see if that new store opened yet?
Rapid Fire	Acts as barriers to a client responding to your inquiry because too much is asked back-to-back	**Worker**: Did you know the boy who was shot at the school yesterday? **Client**: Yes **Worker**: Do you know what happened? **Client**: No **Worker**: Did you feel scared? **Client**: Yes
Double-barreled	When a worker asks multiple questions at once	**Client**: I am so glad I have my license now! **Worker:** Really, when did you pass the test? Do you have a car yet?

Application

EXCERISE 4: You will need to review the *Contracting Video* in MyClasses Canvas. Next, complete the process recording chart for the video and breakdown the usage of questions in the session. In your process recording you will need to identify the following skills and information:

- Type of Question (open, closed)

- What did the worker learn as a result of asking this question?

- Quality of the question (e.g., good, bad). Include what about the question made it good or bad.

- How would you have changed the question if you were conducting the session? (Provide a new question that you could actually ask)

Lesson Five

Ending a Session with a Client

In this lesson we will focus on how we should close a session with a client. With session endings, the assumption is that we will continue to work with this client.

Throughout the session, social workers utilize a variety of skills. Those skills include: non-verbal communication (SOLER skills), attending, listening, summarizing, and utilizing questions. For a social worker to have successful session endings, they have to utilize the abovementioned skills effectively so that they review what has been addressed during the session(s) and then create a plan to move forward.

At the end of each session, the social worker will provide a summary, including strengths, about what was discussed in this session. Then, the social worker will ask for feedback to ensure that the summary is accurate. Finally, the social worker and the client will discuss next steps and will plan for the next session and review any tasks that need to be completed prior to the next session.

This is an important but often overlooked component of social work practice. How we as social workers end the session can set the tone for your next meeting. It is also likely that how you end your sessions can impact your working relationship with a client. For example, if you rush a client out of your office or fail to set up a follow-up meeting before they leave, the client could make assumptions about your level of investment in their change process.

As social workers, we need to reflect on our own thoughts and feelings during and after session endings. The following questions can help us both process our own feelings and think about how to improve our social work skills.

Questions to ask self during and after endings:

- How do I feel about this ending?

- Who can I speak with about my emotions (if needed)?

- What social work skills did I use well?

- What social work skills do I still need to improve upon?

- How can I continue to learn and adapt these skills?

- What can I learn from this professional relationship?

- How can I apply this to other professional relationships?

Application

EXCERISE 5.1: Watch the *Contracting Video* in MyClasses Canvas and pay attention to how the worker ends the session.

Discuss the following prompts:

1. Discuss what was done well by the worker.

2. Identify the skills used by the social worker to help facilitate the ending (e.g. SOLER, summarizing)

3. If you were the social worker in this session, how would you have ended the session with the client in the video?

Application

EXCERISE 5.2: Complete the Mindtool quiz (located in MyClasses Canvas) and answer the following questions:

1. Why do you think it is important for a social worker to communicate clearly with a client, especially as they end/close a session?

2. What was your mindtool quiz score and interpretation?

3. Do you agree or disagree with the interpretation?

4. What is something new you learned about your communication skills from the quiz?

5. What are some strategies you could use to help enhance and grow your communication skills as you move forward in your social work career?

Lesson Six

Documentation Know How

Discussion

Documentation is very important in social work practice. As professional social workers, we document everything that happens with a client. We utilize a number of different documentation tools, including:

- Contact notes – form where you describe your contact with the client (via phone, face to face, etc.)

- Collateral contact notes – form where you describe the contact with someone other than the client (teachers, family member, probation officer, etc.)

- Assessments – initial form used to gather the client's history

- Treatment plans – form where you describe, in detail, the client's goals (sometimes called goal plans, service plans, or intervention plans)

- Release of Information – form utilized to get permission from the client to share their personal, confidential information with others

When writing out documentation it is often helpful to follow the S.O.A.P. format. When following S.O.A.P a worker should be SUBJECTIVE and OBJECTIVE in their documentation. The worker should also provide an ASSESSMENT of the client's functioning and reaction to the interaction with the worker. Finally, the worker should include a PLAN for moving forward.

Each of the different forms of documentation are utilized so we can provide detailed information about our work with our client. When social workers document client's information we strive to make sure that we utilize specific techniques in order to avoid a number of common errors. See the following table for what to include and what to avoid.

Table 6.1

Techniques to Include	What to Avoid
• Person first language • 3rd person language • Client's strengths (Strengths Based Approach) • Quotation marks when you note what the client said • The date that the encounter took place and your signature • Black ink if handwritten or typed • Non-biased language • Grammatically correct English • Clear, specific, and concise sentences • Differentiate between what is a fact and what is your professional impressions. Be sure to include language that introduces your professional impressions	• I, We, Our or You statements • Pencil, white out, or blue ink • Language that your clients do not understand • Professional impressions stated as if they are facts • Biased language (including hostile, offensive, and judgmental language) • Use of Stereotypes (making assumptions about clients)

The following examples will help you better understand what to include and what to avoid.

Table 6.2

Incorrect Way to Document	Correct Way to Document	What Correct Technique Was Used?
The client had unprotected sex with her father and is now pregnant with his child.	Bianca, a 14 year old, African American female was raped repeatedly by her father. Due to these incidents of sexual assault by her father, Bianca is now pregnant with her second child.	• Non-biased language • Clear, specific, and concise sentences
The addict says she wants to change, but she is not telling the truth.	Amy, a person who is currently using illegal substances, stated in our last session that she wanted to stop using heroin. This social worker noticed that this statement contradicts her reported behavior of using heroin last night.	• Person first language • Stating professional impressions • Non-biased language • 3rd person language (when referring to social worker)

Table 6.2 Continued

Incorrect Way to Document	Correct Way to Document	What Correct Technique Was Used?
The client is whining about her current life situation, because she recently learned she is an HIV positive person.	The client expressed sadness and confusion about her recent HIV positive diagnosis. She stated that she "does not know how to cope" and that she "doesn't know how to tell her family".	• Clear, specific, and concise • Quotation marks to identity the client's own words • Non-judgmental language
The client is from Baltimore, MD and so he is likely involved in a gang and has a history of violent behaviors.	The client is from Baltimore, MD.	• Clear, specific, and concise • Non-judgmental language • Avoidance of stereotyping
The clients showed up for their appointment and they were talking loud and ghetto.	The clients presented for their appointment with this worker.	• Clear, specific, and concise • Non-judgmental language

Consider This! Look at Table 6.3. For each of the incorrect documentation statements in the table you will need to write out the correct way to document the client interaction. You will also need to identify what specific techniques were utilized to correct the documentation statement.

Table 6.3

Incorrect Way to Document	Correct Way to Document	What Correct Technique Was Used?
The client seemed to have a hard time expressing himself. I think he might be slow or have some type of learning handicap.		
This mom came in for her session and she had a lot of kids with her and they all had different dads. She asked for help with food and housing but it doesn't seem like she's serious about really helping herself.		
I think the client has low self-esteem and just needs help finding a girlfriend and learning how to be a man.		

Application

EXERCISE 6.1: Assess the quality of writing in the *Example Psychosocial Assessment* <u>on the next page</u>. Answer the following questions.

1. What are some examples of **judgmental** writing from the Psychosocial Assessment example?

2. How could the worker have re-worded those statements in order to be professional and non-judgmental?

3. What are some examples of **biased** language from the Psychosocial Assessment example?

4. How could the worker have re-worded those statements in order to be professional and un-biased?

5. What are some examples of **vague or non-factual** writing from the Psychosocial Assessment example?

6. How could the worker have re-worded those statements in order to be professional and avoid being vague or relying on personal impressions?

EXAMPLE PSYCHOSOCIAL ASSESSMENT

Salisbury Family Service Agency Psychosocial Assessment

Client Name: Brian Taylor   Age:13
Social Worker: Renea Wilkins

Presenting Problem:

Brian Taylor is a 13 year old Caucasian male, who was referred to services by his mom because she felt really worried since her son is acting really strange and angry. The client believes the main solution to his problem is for his parents to get off of his back about his grades. He states, "If I can just get some space at home then I wouldn't be so angry."

Physical Functioning and health:

Brian has been to the doctor regularly and his mother doesn't report any major health concerns for her son. Brian has recently been overeating and has gained weight. This is true because his stomach hangs over his belt a little bit.

Interpersonal and Social Relationships:

Brian has a lot of friends from a lot of different races. His friends are negative and are not a good influence on him. He acts like he doesn't understand why his mom doesn't like his friends.

Religion and spirituality:

Brian does not participate in any church related activities or groups currently. This is probably why he feels so angry. Brian should look into getting involved in a church.

Impression and assessment:

Brian Taylor is a 13 year old Caucasian male, who was referred for services by his mom because she felt really worried since her son is acting really strange and angry. Brian seemed to be feeling pretty happy during our meeting but may have really low self-esteem. Brian and his mom have a lot of conflict and it is probably because she's not home a lot due to working two jobs. The client's appearance was kind of messy and his shoes were kind of dirty but his hair cut was nice and it looked like he had taken a shower today. Brian does have anger issues and needs to work on talking better to his mom. He also needs to get his grades up and find better friends.

Application

EXERCISE 6.2: Using the contact note given (as a guide or to write on directly), create a contact note of the session displayed in the *Intake* Video in MyClasses Canvas. Refer to your readings for examples. Remember to include information on 1) the focus of the session; 2) a summary of the client's behavior, appearance, and affect; 3) any resolution(s) that occur; 4) Any follow-up that will occur

Contact Note

Client Name: **Date of Contact:**

Length of session: _____minutes
Type of Contact: Individual Session
          Telephone
          Family Meeting
          Group Session
          Other contact: _____

_____
_____
_____
_____
_____
_____
_____
_____
_____

Social Worker Signature: _____

Date: _____

Lesson Seven

Professional Social Work Practice

Discussion 7.1 Professional Social Work Attire and Engagement

Professional social workers are knowledgeable about the code of ethics, social work values and principles, and understand the importance of their own behaviors, language, appearance, and non-verbal communication. We realize that all of these areas affect relationships with clients and colleagues.

Many agencies and organizations often have policies related to professionalism. To find out more about these policies within your social work educational program you should refer to the student handbook (e.g. the Salisbury University School of Social Work Technical Standards located within the BASW Program Handbook).

Professionalism includes:

✓ Smiling when we greet clients or colleagues

✓ Allowing our facial expressions to mimic that of our clients (e.g. if they are crying, we do not want to smile)

✓ Refusing to participate in gossip or other degrading conversations

✓ Listening, then speaking

✓ Understanding what knowledge you still need and identifying sources where you can gather that knowledge. Remember, social workers are life-long learners

✓ Willingness to engage in self-reflection

✓ Wearing clothing that is appropriate for your work environment (i.e. if you work/play with children on a regular basis you want to wear clothing that is comfortable and allows you to move throughout the day). If you are unsure if your clothing is appropriate for this job, please ask your supervisor

✓ Utilizing non-biased language both verbally and in writing (e.g. saying that a client is lazy and won't find a job instead of saying that the client is currently unemployed)

✓ Utilizing 'person first' language both verbally and in writing (e.g. writing "autistic client" instead of using person with autism)

✓ Practicing ethical social work practice by following the Code of Ethics and asking questions when unsure about how to handle an ethical dilemma

Professionalism does not include:

- ☒ Gossiping about clients or colleagues

- ☒ Sharing confidential information

- ☒ Speaking without listening

- ☒ Being a "know-it-all" (no one knows everything about every topic!)

- ☒ Wearing clothing that is not appropriate for your work environment

- ☒ Using biased language and/or offensive terms

Avoid wearing:

- ☒ Low cut tops

- ☒ Low pants that show your undergarments

- ☒ Tight fitting clothing

- ☒ Clothes that allow your tattoos to be visible

Application

EXERCISE 7.1: View the "What NOT to Do" video in MyClasses Canvas and answer the following questions:

1. Create a list of unprofessional things you noticed in this video (utilize your readings and the previous lists to help you identify language, behaviors, and appearance concerns).

2. Identify what the worker should have done differently to present as professional.

3. What areas of professionalism might you struggle with? What can you change or implement into your practice as a social work student to help you address these areas?

Discussion 7.2 Self-Awareness and Professional Social Work Practice

As social workers, we have contact with people and situations that are different from our own. Sometimes these situations test our beliefs and values and cause us to have an emotional reaction. How we handle these reactions is so important for us, our clients, our co-workers, and the larger systems that we work within.

In addition to the Code of Ethics, social workers need to be self-aware and possess self-understanding. We need to realize that our worldview (our way of doing things and our values) is not the only option. We also need to recognize when a situation causes feelings from our own personal life to surface that it is not about the client, but instead about us. When this happens, we need to recognize these feelings for what they are: ours. With self-understanding and self-awareness we are able to recognize how our own feelings, values, attitudes, and behaviors shape us as professionals. This insight allows us to be able to effectively help others.

Application

EXERCISE 7.2: This self-awareness activity provides you the opportunity to reflect on the specific types of clients you are comfortable working with and who it might be difficult to work with as a social worker. For this activity, *you will need to pick four of the statements provided.* For each statement you choose write out if you would be comfortable or uncomfortable working with the clients discussed. You should also provide an explanation as to why you would feel comfortable or uncomfortable working with the client. It is very important to be honest while doing this activity. Remember, you are not being asked if you would want to work with this client or not, instead it is about your level of comfort.

1. A 29 year old man, with three young children who refuses treatment for a life threatening illness because his religion prohibits him from getting help

2. A 50 year old adult male who will not speak with his son because he recently found out his son was gay

3. A same sex couple that wants your help to adopt a child

4. A woman, currently in the hospital with many broken bones, who will not leave her husband because she took a wedding vow that she would be an obedient, faithful, and loving wife

5. A young woman who wants an abortion and is seeking your help to find doctors who will do the procedure

6. A 15 year old young woman who is converting to Islam, and wants your help with how to navigate the change of wearing the Hijab

7. A father, who refuses to see his grandchild because that grandchild is his daughter's child, but born via insemination and adopted by his daughter's lesbian partner

8. A mother, who identifies as Catholic and refuses to let her daughter leave the house, except for school, because the daughter identifies as Wiccan

9. A mother who is court ordered to do supervised visits with her children after allegations of physical abuse and neglect against her 2 and 3 year old children were substantiated